The Shady Sisters

The Shady Sisters

poems

NANCY MEANS WRIGHT

WindRidge
BOOKS

Cover Art:
John Singer Sargent, The Brook, 21½ x27 in.,
Private Collection. Photo courtesy Adelson Galleries, NY.
Cover and book design by Laurie Thomas

ISBN: 978-1-944485-10-8
Library of Congress Control Number: 2016935556

Published by Wind Ridge Books, an imprint of
Voices of Vermonters Publishing Group, a nonprofit literary
arts organization in Shelburne, Vermont, USA.

www.windridgebooks.org

For my large, loving family: all of you out there
who gave birth to this collection of poems.

And in memory of my mother Jessie
and my sister Grace.

how sister gazed at sister
reaching through mirrored pupils
back to the mother   —*Adrienne Rich*

Of two sisters one is always the watcher,
one the dancer.   —*Louise Gluck*

Contents

Three

Four

How Our Scots Grandmother Got Her Red Hair *

He lay in the tatters of his wolf skins, a half-mile
from our grandmother's birth place
by the River Leven: a grinning skull in a rusted
helmet, rude round shield on the rib-cage, fusty sword,

and a pair of crusted fish hooks caught in his clavicle
where once his beard grew thick and braw.
Norsemen left their memoirs largely in the pelt
and whiskers—plenty of red in those: a link

from Norse to Scotland's South: my sonsie,
ancestral lass—to us. Did he catch her in the rashes
or did she consent to the wink of a wild copen e'e
and claret hair like straw in a wind-blaw? A moment,

perhaps, of something beyond lust, as I felt
at the unexpected kiss from the shy, sky-eyed lad
in eighth grade. Then waited for a call that never
came. Though he never left Leven, did he, this

dashing young warrior. Slain in his prime, I suspect,
by an angry father, who later sent the lass full-
bellied like a Viking sail to a tenable port. Where she bore
a redhaired bairn and called her Derdriu. For *sorrow*.

*After a 1263 raid on the western port of Largs, Norsemen fled toward the
North Sea, via the River Leven. Derdriu is a tragic heroine in Ulster-Scots
mythology*

Annie's Lament

(after Rembrandt)

John Mayne is sunk in his chair like an old
boat, sails ragged and out of wind,
reeking of onions, garlic and bird droppings,
the cargo it carries. The balding head,
flung back to the light from a window he'll
never see again, the callous hands
knotted in prayer: *Sorry I am*, he bleats,
for accusing *me*, Annie, of selling the goat
when all along it was the hired lad
stole into the byre that night. Ach, so
little trust between us.
                         The husband's
not sorry, no. Even the wee mutt springs
to greet me, lick my toes, sniffing cat—
but not John, no—only the pointing finger:
You put him up to it.
                        All those aching years
I worked on this hardship farm.
The old man whining, absorbed in *self*,
while I, like a thousand other Ulster
wives, wed too young, scour the house,
concoct a meal of mutton, shrunken potato,
gruel he'll slop on his lap and then complain
I starve him—him! When truth is,
the hunger is *mine*—watching that bibulous
old bloat rock and rock all day
at its mooring, with no destination in sight.

Sharks

Mother sits in a yellow canvas chair
under a red-striped umbrella.
She wears a black-skirted bathing suit,
her russet hair is pulled back
in a frazzled braid, her toes warm the sand.
A *Life* magazine spreads her lap.
                                                She
gazes out to sea where water
meets a pallid sky, where clouds
shadow a passing ship, and a year ago
a swimmer lost a leg to a shark—
and she thinks of her son in his war.
She has memorized last week's
report:
            Your son, wounded in action.
She tries to visualize *wounded*,
but comes up with sharks, their silvery-
dark fins, their long sleek bodies
angling through the waters. Razor teeth—
that awful beauty.
                            Billions of
years ago, she thinks, her ancestors swam
this sea, wary of sharks but sensing
kinship, the wildness they shared. Wildness
she knew in her own Scots grandmother
who once struck a man so hard when
he cheated on her daughter, he was
blinded. Wildness in the fist
she shakes now at this war—at the men
who began the war. At the dark place
in her heart that informs her what
they are. What *she* is.

Sallie Mayne Takes Ship for the Land of Plenty

When you took that ship from Derry
even in the wake of the one that
foundered in sight of land
like a stick boat filled with folk
whose skin stretched like hide over the ribs
of a curragh, rocking their porous bones
and keening for family they'd
never in this wide world see again;

    when as a single mum of twenty-one
you waved at the shrinking shore
as though you'd be back on the fortnight,
bowels threatening to spill
into your broken shoes, and sailed
on a ship meant to carry twelve thousand
gallons of water but held only
a fraction of that in leaking casks
like a damp dream, and thirty berths
for three hundred reeking bellies;

    when there were only rats for meat,
uncaulked timbers and rotten rigging,
filth beyond the match of metaphor; eight
starved weeks to cross a sea cruel as
a stranger knocking you down a gangway;
fifty companions fed to sharks, another
hundred lousy with fever, your sweet
babe sick, her soul surrendered to hell—

    well, did you ever imagine,
Sallie Mayne, you'd one day be the great-
great-grand-mum of fat-cheeked bairns
complaining they've got to eat their p'tatoes
before they can taste their apple pie?

Our Grandmother's Bust

The statue sat in the crook of the stair:
it had pointy ears and a smirk
that wrinkled its porcelain nose. We were

scared as kids to climb the steps so Gran
kept a potty for us below. We thought it
the devil, and Grandfather called it the bust

of an Irish priest. No dancing. No foolish
games. No idle talk in *his* house. It was
only after an uncle came to visit we found

it was Dionysus—horns and flute, all
but the hooves. I thought I heard our Gran one
night on the dusky stair, her tongue lapping

the statue's lips, howling past the study
where Grandfather scored in scarlet the sins
of his congregation. The night whispered

its incomprehensible secrets into my ears
until I wriggled my body deep down
in the quilts and sleep took away the dark.

In the morning there was Gran in the kitchen,
buttering the old man's toast, a thin, reedy
glee whistling through her big gap-teeth.

The Cottar Weavers
of Leven Fifeshire

Meg sleeps with her sisters in the weaving
room. It's nearly dawn, and the linen threads
stretch on the hand-looms like a hundred tedious
lives: brown ochre black—the dark breath

hurries her heart. Up in the loft, Father rolls
off the passive mother, warp over weft,
creaking their box bed. A sibling elbow
cautions Meg; the cumbrous boots descend

and she pulls the patchy blanket close.
Her fingers are raw as unbleached flax,
her shoulders pinch like second-hand shoes.
The body shrinks from its extremities.

The caged bird warbles at the first small
light: the twelve-hour work day looms.

Jemima Is Her Own Marketplace

She leans on the iron railing, broad-
hipped Scot in hand-me-down boots,
    squints into the world:
    shouts *Jemmy's Market,*
    six steps up! Cries
ballades in buckets and lays

from her boned flesh. Apples
and guilt from her breasts,
    cream from the nipples,
    grief from the gut,
    and want from her
empty purse. She'll sell her verse

dear, our agoraphobic forebear:
there will be no giving away.
    While down in the streets
    where the stones kick
    at the heels of the lax
and lamps hang from their stalks

like thieves, the shoppers pass in
silence. But look! a lady in pink
    calls for a villanelle—
    and thrilled—though
    quivering to contemplate
descent, Jemmy takes a step

down like a thin person pushed
into cold water. The carroty hairs
    bristle on her scalp;
    she hangs in balance,
    a small weight—till panic
implodes desire—and she dashes

back up. *Wait!* Too late. The pink
lady's gone. She sucks in a breath
    and waits for the next:
    a black wool look-
    out on a shaky rise,
wall-eyes winking her rotten luck.

Aunt Jo Takes on the Therapist

Aunt Jo's got the only rocking chair
and won't rock. Nurse says *the honeymoon
is up*; says *every body moves
in this establishment.* Jo thinks, *unfair,*
sits mum as a dummy, moustache aflare
under the waxy nose. Sly Yankee,
she didn't run a meat mart forty cranky
years for this.
                    And no Scotch? Unbear-
able. *Pigheaded,* Nurse declares;
*she'll root her way into a state home,
then she'll be sorry. Up, Love, and show
us how. Last chance.*
                    But love's a stone.
Stiff as a frozen slab of pork, thumbs
up, Jo's carried out: won
                    or done.

Life In the Presbyterian Forties

1
Our Scots-Irish daddy is picking apples.
His orange tie snags on a splintered twig,
he flicks off a maggot. He'd rather be
at Kenny's Bar or yelling at the Brooklyn
Dodgers but Mother is baking pies
for the kirk—Mother, who was taught
to hold her tongue, who'd rather be reading
a book. The oven sweats while the crust
rolls out on the cutting board. She'll lace
the apples with sugar, a verse from Genesis,
a pinch from an adder's tongue.

2
Our dreamer dad is bemused. He swivels
on his tilted ladder, he flies into
his fancy. Thumps Mother with a green
to the hip, a rotting red to the breast
and back she fires—smack on the Ulster nose!
*Then the eyes of both were opened,
and they knew they were naked.* ★
Husband and wife pitch and heave
till the tree is bare of fruit and the ladder
collapses into a pool of apple pulp.

3
Mother warns from the window
and Daddy picks faster and Mother
shoves one-two-three pies into the oven.
A maggot grins in an apple core.
We fold our hands on the scarified table
as Mother whispers the evening
prayer: *Praise Him who gives food to
all flesh...* My sister and I feed
on the fruits of our parents' compliance.
The quiet cancer of their godly works.

★*Genesis:3-7*

13

The Shady Sisters

live in a house with yellow shutters
    and yellow doors. I suspect

that the wallpaper is yellow too,
    but I've never been inside.

A yellow sign on the yellow porch
    says the Shady Sisters

make lampshades to specification.
    And they do. I know because one day

my husband went in and came out
    a cut-out, thirteen-inch lampshade.

Now every night when I switch
    on the light by my pillow

Gilbert grins down through the holes
    in the cut-out shade

but he can't speak.
    Thanks to the Shady Sisters

I am able to finish my writing
    without interruption.

Two

Before the Freeze

This morning the girl can see clear
to the bottom of the pond,
pebbles like glass eyes and fish
flashing cut quartz.
                              Out in the center
a duck floats, still, as though
painted onto the surface; feathers extend
the waters. Wind ribs the girl's hair
over her eyes, the world purls
and puckers.
                              Tomorrow the boy
in the book on her lap will drown.
There is no way out,
she already knows the ending.
                              Tonight
there will be a frost, the ice
will creep up like a feral cat to seize
the duck. Its head is nacre green,
the breast a russet leaf that breathes
in the soft swell as though
it would suck up the day, the hour,
the instant.
                              The girl lies back
on the grassy bank, her toes dig the dirt,
her hands cradle her neck and the book
drops into the weeds.
                              She floats
in the lap of autumn currents. Her chest
expands with each quick breath.
The sun is hot on her damp green brow.

Flight

There they are: a clutch of peregrine falcon
chicks chipping their way back out of a DDT
wasteland and onto the Deerleap Cliff
of the Bristol Ledges, a rock face crumbled
into niches for nesting, far above the jays,
grouse, and sleepy-eyed juncos who
nestle below, like the girl on the meadow's edge.

Drawn by the birds, she climbs the rocks
to watch as the young take flight, as the wide,
opulent wings wheel out over the ridge,
as they stroke through tides of wind as though
they've some rough destination in mind.
Then touched with gold in the last slow
spill of sun, they vanish upward into fire.

Giddy, alone, on the darkening crag, Ruth
stands motionless, unable to move.
Her head and breast burn with a fever heat
she has never before known—even
in flight on the narrow wooden swing
from the apple tree, or on the plane her pilot
brother steered through a fleet of clouds.

She knows it is getting late: she must find
the way down again; it's the only way
for her. She walks quickly, kicking aside
the choke of vines, stones and roots.
Her arms flail like rude wings; her
legs bowl her waxing body down,
down to collapse into a cold March muck.

Christmas Eve Service in the City

A small-bellied buddha, chest bent
to her spindly knees, the child squints
at the cardboard manger: Jesus soon to be
nailed ankle, knuckle-bone to a cross.
He died to save you, the black-frocked

pastor moans while the girl, brought
here to church by Grandmother, squats
in the moment, elbows crushed
to her kid sister's ribs like Dad's best
Sunday pants caught in a press.

Her eyes fix on the sugary canes that
hang like red-striped fruit on the balsam
boughs but no one touches. *Today's
gifts*, the pastor says, *are for baby
Jesus.* The church is cold like the snowy

castle in one of her picture books.
Even Grandmother pulls her black wool
collar up over her bowed shoulders.
Ruth thinks of the throbbing woodstove
home in the Vermont kitchen, the altar

above her mother's creaky wardrobe,
the shiny brown wooden Buddha
plump as a woodchuck in its winter hole.
In twelve weeks, her mother told her,
the beastie—or was it the Buddha? will dig

its way up into the light. Clutching
the white lit candle that Grandmother
placed in her hands and closing her eyes,
Ruth can feel the sun skitter
across her temples. Like footprints.

Teasing

After school got out and there wasn't much to do
before summer camp or lessons at the pool,
the neighbor kids would sometimes go and tease shy
Billy Pratt, or plump Edie Elkins who lived next
door to me—just to see them react. Edie's mother was
straight as a ruler and wouldn't let her leave the yard so
they'd often wander over to hers—and I'd go, too.
                                        At first
she liked the attention. Pat would bring his pet snake
and Jimmy would push her on the swing—so high she'd
go chalk-white—but she didn't cry. And Jimmy said
that was no fun: *Let's find a way to make her.*
Pushing her face in the mud didn't do it or the names
we called her: *Birdbrain Fatso Mama's Baby Ass.*
So Jimmy flung a butterfly net over her head, Barb
and Ted pulled down her pants and held
her so we could all look.
                          And she didn't cry.
One afternoon Mother sent me over with a cherry tart
for Mrs. Elkins—she wasn't home. Her father
was. He was a small man with eyes like shiny nickels.
He gave Edie and me chocolate ice cream, he
played magician. He pulled a fake spider out of my hair,
then a pink butterfly. I smiled. He said he had
a third leg—did I want to see it? Edie knew the trick,
he said: *You stay in the kitchen, Edith.* I followed him
down the hall and he shut the door. He showed me.
I turned and ran. Edie was in the kitchen
on her knees, crying.
                      I waited till she stopped—
I didn't know what to say, except *leave her
alone* when the gang came back that day
to tease her. Jimmy yelled *why?* and I bared my teeth.
Go, I said, *just...go. Go!* And they all went.

Breach of Promise

Daddy kneels, rump up, in the broomy
grass of our back yard, his balding
head bent to the rusty hand mower—

something gone wrong again. Sweat
bubbles his brow; the slow decay
of roses creeps into the clefts

of the kitchen window. *He acts,*
Mother says, gripping her hands,
like a man about to be beaten. Have it

mowed, Rob, she shouts, *they're*
coming at five. I rub her shoulders: *Mom,*
he'll fix it—he'll get it done.

She points next door at Foleys' lawn,
pristine-green and shaved close
as a monk's scalp, gasps as our collie

Nell romps up to bump Daddy's butt;
he pitches forward—a wrench
flies out of his hand and into the brush.

He throws up his arms as though he's
given up altogether on broken machines
and rolls in the leaves with Nell. Over

and over they roll, man and dog, laughing
and barking, as if they're in love
with the leaves, in love with each other.

I long to go out and gambol with them, only
I can't leave mom in the kitchen, can I? slicing
grapes and scallions into a dish of cold fruit.

Stranger

Tonight is counselors' night. The tennis coach croons an off-key duet with the swim instructor. The camp nurse pokes a cardboard needle into the swimmer's butt—we collapse with laughter. A chorus girl prances on like a dancing mare: you can see her fleshy thighs as she kicks up high. Fred the riding teacher lifts her into his horsey arms; her red silk skirt swirls about her waist. He trots her across the stage like one of his fillies and she flings up a giddy arm. The piano crescendos as she lopes off with fuzz-cut Fred.

And back she comes. Alone.

It's Mother! She curtsies, her hair shimmies orangey-red under the lights. Mother: a smooth-thighed stranger in black net stockings, holding up her arms to all of us out here in the shadowy circus of chairs. I want to get to know her. I want her to know me. I want to be the only one she holds out her arms to.

Gone. Now only the camp director with a black hat like a bent stovepipe—a white-rag rabbit. He drops the rabbit into the hat. He slaps the hat back on his head. When he takes it off again—there is no rabbit.

No swim instructor, no hairy riding teacher with his red silk mare. There is only the camp director's balding head as he nods to the applause, the hairs like burnt roots on the shiny scalp.

Ropes

Summer nights in quiet Ocean Grove,
they would rope off the streets at six o'clock
and we would go over to the big tent
to watch the evangelicals
weep in the aisles in praise of the lord.
Or warn of abysmal ends if we
misbehaved.
                    Mornings you'd find
the believers on the beach, buttered
and oiled on their sleepy towels or pale-
necked under their tipsy umbrellas.
While down by the water
we'd hang on to the ropes that stretched
shore to sea, and when the waves came
crashing we'd screech as loud
as any born-again. Yet
                         what if the rope
broke—and swept us bad girls out
to sea: mouths, nose, ears swamped, only
frayed ends in our hands? Then
the sharks would come—for the sharks
were out there waiting, patient as Job,
our pious uncle said. One crunch
of the snaggy jaws, he warned, we'd
  be lunch.
              Yesterday in the windy surf
we quarreled, you and I, Ruth, over a boy
I'd met in the lifeguard stand:
he winked, I smiled—you called him *bad*—
and that old wave came plunging up
over my head with such force I thought
I saw the sharks: razor jaws yawning there
in the deep. I cried out, lost my balance,
and the rope let go of my hands.
                         It was

the boy, not you, Neme-sis, who
leapt from his perch and towed me, blubbering,
like a slow, oblique boat, to anchor.

Collage: Mother, Daughter, and Book

Ruth sits in our grandmother's
rocker, nursing her child.
Her bare feet creak the pair
back and forth on splintered legs.
Her unsunned breast glows
in the afternoon light
like a crescent moon;
her nipple is a milky peak
that the child, full of itself,
lets go: it sleeps now
in a crater of her flesh.

The mother is wide awake.
Her arms embrace the child
but one hand holds a book; her head
thrusts forward as if to ward off
guilt and she reads. I know
from the way the book quivers
in her hands, and the green eyes
narrow like a river racing
underground, that she is far
away, at sea; she is pumping
herself up with oysters, she is
breeding pearls in her pap.

Soon she will feed it
to the child. But in these few
moments while her daughter sleeps,
she thinks only of her book
like a parched woman gulping
from a cup with both hands—
and the milk spills,
unnoticed, on the child's cheek.

My Sister Is Drying Green Beans

she sits on a kitchen chair, her jeans
are stained from cranberries,
her legs spread wide into a roomy lap.
An infant sleeps at her breast
in a flowered sack, the head drops down
like a soft brown bird.
      She works
swiftly to shell the beans
before the child wakes;
her arms curve about the sack
like a dancer's. The casings
peel away like cracked leather gloves
but inside, the bean is pale
as the newborn's thumb.
The beans heap up quickly, they
almost reach the child's toes.
Soon they'll dry, they'll keep six
months in a lidded jar—
one winter day Ruth will fix a rich
leguminous meal.
      I'm sunk
in a time warp to watch her, my empty
hands crook in my lap, the skin
splits at the knuckles. I think
of the small white bones inside and
what they've held.
      What they've let go.

Crossing the Ice

This is the shortest way across,
here where Lake Champlain curves
back on itself and into East Creek;
the bridge would add an extra twenty
miles and weddings won't wait.
The rainbow sky dazzles the eye
as we weave among the fishing shacks.

I think of the fish in their dreamy waters
rising for bait like cats after
a glittery bit of moon (my Buddhist
sister's marriage to a much older man—
we are always crossing thin ice).
Already the tires bog down
in the afternoon thaw, and to lighten

the family load I walk, my feet
dumb in my boots, my head afloat
in space. The car is a beacon
ahead of me now, it rushes to shore
like Saturn reeling inside its rings of ice.
Hurry, my mother shouts,
and I take the final yards at a dead shuffle.

Behind, the fishermen are pulling the last
of the shanties off the shrinking ice;
tonight they'll salt the fish, they'll spin
tales around the fire: how *down-lake*
a Volvo broke through the ice
but the foolhardy folks got out. Like us
on the far side now, toasting the bride. Alive.

First Snowfall

Thrilled with the first December down-
rush of snow, my daughter runs out, coatless,
to lie on her back; her eyes and mouth
fill with thick wet flakes. She sweeps her thin
arms in and out, in…out, the muscles taut
as though stroking the oars of the rubber
rowboat we keep on our summer lake.
For a moment she laughs at the furrows
she has carved—or should I say wings—

for already she envies the birds at our feeder.
Even as she goes on rotating her arms,
the fluting fills with snow like a hand scribbling
a new text on top of the old, and the image is
gone. Shaking snow like a wet puppy,
the girl comes slowly in. She stamps her feet
by the woodstove, arms still circling. But
not for warmth—her eyes are fixed on the frosted
window glass as though she'd see through the rime

a lost reflection there. I don't know what to say
except *I'll run you a hot tub, okay?* But
her arms keep on whirling like the snow that is
falling faster, deeper now, burying rocks
and bushes, even the old red wheelbarrow
I forgot to put away. I think of the lost world
of Pompeii: the frozen figure of a child kneeling
on its mother's lap, chin high, hands lifted
as if to forge an open passageway, up into the light.

Cicada Invasion

They've taken over the countryside
like ballpark fans broadcasting
a win after seventeen years
of rout. Everywhere they
shout: that high persistent note:
in trees, shrubs, iris, even my hair
where they dive from husk-heavy
boughs. They sweep the yard
on wickery wings; ogle their mates
on my damp hung sheets—
a last rite of the dead, an orgy
of coloraturas; a grappling
of wings, bellies, limbs, a spew
of eggs. A mass grave—no one to close
those ruby eyes. Oh
but the nymphs will hatch, they will
burrow back into the earth,
they will suck on the honeyed roots.
They will wait. They will wait.

What is it like to live underground,
invisible to the world? Is it
simply a long nap, like a bat in its winter
cave? A girl in a *hijab* kept
from school, mute as a frozen
bulb? Or a foetus, snug in the womb,
waiting for waters to break?
Like my zen buddhist sister, yes, who
sang to the crowning head
of her newborn: *Welcome back, child!*
I, too, would cry out at that
first onrush of light. I would strip
to the skin, I would dance till I dropped.
I would lay my future in eggs.

Piano Concert

You expect more of her because
she is tall for eight years
and my daughter knows this. You can
almost hear the bones click in her hips
as she scurries across the stage
in patent leather shoes like
a runner bent on the winner's tape,
and thumps down on the hard bench.
There is something feral in the way
she lifts her hands to crook
her fingers—a kitten waiting
to pounce; the eyes are green slits
in the blade of her face. She
begins, her hands slow weights
on the keys. You hold your breath.
Mozart seems to elude her until
she leans her whole body into the hunt,
plays with the music, lets go, snatches it
back, her spine twists and stretches.
She's giddy now with flight, rout,
pursuit, wants only quarry. At last
she lays it on you, leaps up and bows:
a fall of bright hair masks her eyes.
You blink and she's gone,
the music, still, in your ears.

Waiting for a News Break

Fay's man is out of work and now he
has quit shaving: he's Scrooge
in a nightshirt till noon; he's a fat
whiskery cat snoozing in a black
leather chair. The dailies drift
around him, scuzzy as last week's
snow. He'll shovel them into bags
along with the empty wine bottles—

eventually. Nights though,
like the housewife dressing
to greet the plumber, he still wakes
to the news. Lehrer, Rather,
Simon—he gulps them down
with his chopmeat, spoons them up
with his pudding. He knows it's
the same old news, he knows how

things repeat; he has outlived a war
and an ex-wife, borne too many
friends' coffins (he says) to recount.
Still there may be something
he missed: a scandal at the Vatican,
a coup in the White House.
A cache of nukes in Iran, Osama
bin Laden captured, taking a leak.

Like his own foundering flesh
there is always a rise or
a fall somewhere. When it comes
he wants to be on the breaking wave,
he wants to be swept up in
the hi-jacked plane as it screeches
toward shore, as it crashes onto the beach,
as it caves into the swamped sand.

The Conversation

(after a painting by Henri Matisse)

Homo erectus stands in striped
pajamas, hands jammed into his pockets
as if carrying his sex there
like a handful of change—while she, taut
in a blue chair, lifts a swan neck,
hands like caught fish in her lap,
hair ruled by an oval ear
as if it's her only instrument
of speech. The eyes are a black mask.

How did Matisse know to paint us
into this picture? You and I like most
folk at an art show: so many riches—
a six-course dinner. One eats
into the next and appetite's
gone. He's probably only asking why
she forgot to buy toothpaste—what
can she say? She hadn't noticed. Or
maybe what she wants is a way back to Eden
but now she's stuck in a blue-black
canvas, her mouth stopped with paint.
Her eyes, like mine, pleading *Hear me!*

Harvest Moon over Boys' Home

Tonight the moon hangs fat as a full
belly over the Home for Boys at the end
of our road and the lads are feeling
its pull. One by one, they crawl out
of their cots, down the cranky steps
and into the luminous wood to breathe in
the ferns, the witch's broom,
the sugar maple leaves. Coons rustle
the brush, a beaver slaps its tail
by the running brook while flying squirrels
hustle the moon and gold-eyed wolves
and mother bears swaddle their cubs.

But these boys have no mothers.
No fathers—unless you count the priest
who drops in once a month to hear
their sins. *You won't run away again, boy?*
No, Father, I swear it. Yet tonight
they hunt the moon until it slides
between the oaks, and the chill creeps in
like slivers of glass and when
the men come running to bring them
home, the boys surrender, and follow.

While back in the den, cubs suck
on the black gum nipples; the heat
of their dreamy bodies will keep them
alive through the long bear winter.

Digging Up an Old Wound

Tearing down a derelict garage,
my neighbor turns up a brood
of ten: mother and babies wrapped
like plums in a pouch. Possibly
dead, a macabre grin on her pointy
face—a smell like a gas pipe leak.
Scaly-tailed as a lizard, she might've
crawled out of
                        a nightmare:
The neighbor's lips pucker
as if he's dug such things before
and they get in the way of pouring
cement—who wants a putrefaction
of possums in his foundation?
                                    Still

I'm glad when the rain holds
off the digging. I need to come
to grips with these beasts
that once hung by a tail, wrapped
now around a concrete block—
and Mom a double-wombed home-
maker, pumping out thirty
to my one.
                Imagine that journey
up the belly, birth canal
to pouch: blind as a raisin, a pink
astronaut on tether, and only
thirteen teats.
                    All at once these
survivors of yet another upheaval
alive! riding the mother's back
as she dashes over the stone wall
headed for Route 7:
                        like myself six
years in the nuptial nest, not
looking at the dead thing in my heart,
praying it's only playing possum.

Narrow Escape

She drives into a frieze of blue hills,
peel of ochre paint on Longey's store,
Bronson's boats off-keel: across
from the white church the Foote Sisters'
stand of snap beans; swerves
before an oncoming Dodge
into Cider Mill Road—the Adirondacks
fall faint in the West.

Apple trees twist on their roots
at the old place: Sheep's Nose grafted
onto MacIntosh—will it take?
Blackeyed Susan and Sweet Brier
in the driveway: the stalled tractor, pickup
parked sideways, no room for the blue Subaru.
Inside, the horsehair sofa shocks,
piles of old newspapers, sink still leaks;
the tiger cat rubs her legs, wanting
food: Fay bends to the habit. On the table
a woman's straw hat, curtains
new in the windows—kill the view.

She packs her books: Edgeworth, Woolf,
Wollstonecraft, old romances picked up
in second hand bookstores. Steals
upstairs, a ghost in blue denim, grabs
a quilt, wicker wastebasket, white linen
sheets they'd lain on (she walked out bare
handed). Quiet in the attic thick as old
blankets, the sweater her grandmother wore
against the sea winds ripped on the edges:

she winds it close. Her shoulder bones
squeeze as she gropes her way down again,
down where the cat squeals, wind gutters, old

boards creak *step on a crack, you're dead.*
The screen door bangs on her heels.
She halts. Something left behind?
Never mind. Already she tastes salt. Fay's off.

Acrophobia

Fay's reading Virginia Woolf: how
a woman ought to have five hundred
pounds and a room of her own. Fay's got
the room all right—six flights up and over

looking Video King. If you lean out
the bathroom window you can see a slice
of sky and sometimes the handle
on the Dipper. But Fay's got acrophobia.

Open the window: her knees quake, belly
wheezes, blood leaks into her knuckles
and Fay collapses in a bang of bones.
Still Woolf holds something for Fay: how

many middle-aged women walk out with
only a sack on the back, rocks in the pocket—
where's the five hundred pounds now?
So Fay sticks stars on the bathroom ceiling,

half moon over the toilet, *To the Lighthouse*
next to the Zinfandel by the four-legged tub;
red gloxinia in the window and snap-
shots of the family in each cracked

pane. When Fay gets a yen for the Dipper
she looks at those faces: one has the grin
Fay wore in school the time she told them
her Uncle Frank was F.D.R. in the White House.

For a whole week until they found out
Fay was the big kid in town. Fay was a star
on the ceiling. Fay was a room of her own.
A room with a rusted lock, a missing key.

Comeback

Once again forsythia
flings up its fandango arms
and hyacinth blows
purple breath
into April air
while inside on the couch
my man sleeps
as he sleeps away his
days now. And yet

a book stands perfectly up-
right in his hands
as though it would flip
a page of itself
and carry on the waning life
the way an old-time
player might stroll
onto the stage in yellow satin
to usher in a new act.

Tableau

Three o'clock in the morning
    and under a full white moon
a doe twists off the woody
    limbs of a yellow birch.
She is haunch-deep
    in snow, her skin is ribbed
like a thin woven creel;
    a fawn lifts on its slender
legs beside her to nibble
    the raggedy slips
of rhododendron.

    A man watches from a window:
the waist of his beige pajama
    is pinned to keep it
from falling, his hands hang
    like twigs from the bony wrists.
The kidneys have killed
    his desire, though not his
need for food. They stand
    together in the globe
of the winter moon as though
    the man, too, is splitting
the shoots of the yellow birch
    and I am the lone
watcher at the window.

    The doe has her young,
our daughter is gone
    from the house and I have
only the starved man
    who raps now on the glass,
and deer and man,
    as my husband has willed it,
vanish into shadows.

Choices

My daughter is feeding Robert Frost
to her father. He lies in bed
in a coma, his mouth opened wide
as though he would swallow the words
into his laboring lungs: *long I stood*
And looked down one as far as I could...

The patient gives no clue to the looking.
The eyes are shut that once imagined
the green of a Galway wood. *He is*
making his choice, Allie cries, and she runs
from the house with a knowing glance,
out into the road: *I doubt if I should ever*

come back! she shouts over a shoulder.
The sun catches her wilding hair
like a child's fist at hide n'seek; she is
steaming along now, she is searching
for answers she can't find in this room
where her father pushes his shallow

wind in and out, in and out, in and
out. There are no answers. There is only
my daughter. She is almost
around the bend now, her heels kick
pebbles and fallen twigs; in my mind's ear
I can hear the quick, live, breath.

Saying Goodbye To
a Daughter Heading East

Eighteen, and my daughter is off to seek
Enlightenment, green

Nikes on her sturdy feet, a red ruck-
sack strapped to her slender back—

I think of a leafcutter ant relaying
a chunk of apple fifty times its weight.

She's bound for Katmandu, my Allie,
who's never travelled more than forty miles

from home. *The end is the journey,*
she quotes—as though the brown burnished

Buddha in her pack will carry her,
safe, through this *best of possible worlds.*

We both know better about *best*
but we don't say it. We em-

brace goodbye as the afternoon
sun turns the airport windows to webs

of glittery gauze, coaxing my daughter
into its *fata morgana.* We tear apart.

Allie shrinks in my
watch as she sprints through the widening gateway.

Stealing Home to Starksboro

I choose the river road, closer to home
but longer—the road bends
like pins crushed in my salty hair.
Ahead the Bristol Cliffs lure the eye
away from the road—I brake, and the sun
spills into the brook, soaks the clouds
pink, the rocks turn indigo. I'm
giddy with the musk of manure, hay
steaming up into blue silos, corn
squealing on windy stalks—I want to howl
in the harvest.
                Now the road twists
sharp, up into the pass; the mountain
sheds light like a woman peeling
off her clothes for bed. Trees shiver
in wrinkled skins, dark devours
the evergreens, the long curving climb
cramps my engine. How did I end
here alone on a mountain? Light's on
in the kitchen, the cat mewls at my heels:
cat and woman wanting *in*.

Bullfrogs at the Round Barn
in Waitsfield

At the Round Barn Farm
  Eine Kleine Nachtmusik
rushes toward rondo: the cello

leans, a lover, into its strings;
    the violin darts arrows,
viola's chin nods yes! yes! yes!

to each flying note.
    Listeners on blankets
with citronella lanterns

    we skate on our heads
in the pond while Pekin ducks
    interlace our mirrored feet

in a water ballet—the clucking
    underscores the serenade.
Now the bullfrogs belch

    like glutted giants,
grumble and retch; echo
    the swelling of music

with gutteral gulps as if to insist
    Mozart was an upstart—
before concord was cacophony,

    a crack and grind, crunch,
a growl of the wild. Until
    the reeds pipe up

from some ancient swamp
    and stars pull at our springs.
My sister and I sit silent,

    wriggle our stiffening limbs.
We long now for some-
    thing we can't name.

A Mother Considers Her Pregnant Daughter

My daughter is dividing: she spins
an invisible thread from her belly,

and another, and another until she
is her own twin. Like the orb
weaver, my daughter is the eye

of an elastic world. She sees
through a web darkly. What she

can't see, though, she feels, and so
my daughter hatches a trap, a zig-
zag of sticky silk that reels me

in. And I'm stuck.
It's the way you feel when

the Looptheloop you're riding suddenly
stops
at the very top and the earth

is a million wind-
falls away…and oh God,

I'm frozen shut. She is waiting,
my daughter, she is wrapping me
in silk until she ceases

dividing. Then she'll
deliver me to her off-spring

and I'll thrill to the bond
the way you laugh
out loud when the panicky

spiral is over, and you stagger
off on quaking feet into the grass.

Spring Birches

Each of the two white birches in my yard
grows black mammae

on its bark like a six-breasted Kali—
goddess, my skeptical sister says,

of power. And of *ruin*. Never mind:
the hide is soft as old rags. I lean

on a springy trunk; my weight sets
the leaves a-shimmy like my cat when I

stroke her and she wriggles her
furry head against my leg to leave

her scent. Wind purrs through the leaves
and a thousand silvery beads chime

on Kali's belly. Her limbs reach out
to the next tree, and the next

till the whole copse rings:
ivory-black paps whistling in the quick

June breeze, Kali giving suck
like myself, decades ago

out in the yard, feeding my new-
born among the milky leaves.

The Sisters Go on Holiday in the Auld Country

The morning is gray with our differences:
coming across the Sound of Sleat
we even quibbled over the island's shape—
like wings, I said; you argued *pincers*.
Now it's the bowl you bought in Oban,
a thing of spalted wood, of splits
and gouges that's not for filling,
you insist, but *full of its own story*.
I veer off into a landscape
pocked with the peat hags of our great-
grandmother's day, the roads so scant
that only sheep can pass abreast.
                                        Now
a lorry racketing toward us—I
spin into an elbow of earth that rises—then
drops—a windscatter of grit.
A passing place, yes, you say, *but dammit,
you almost killed us! Didn't you
see him blink his lights?*
                                        Tonight we're
here in old Jessie's berth: the room
is clean and dark, the walls a wrangle
of sea-green shapes that bump
over the cracks and join askew at the seams.
We stare out the window, elbows
touching—*like wings*, I tease,
but you're too drowsy to differ.
                                        Toward dawn
I wake to a gathering of light: greenish-
blue and canny, it comes like eyes
through the shadowy glass—your soft
snoring hardly disturbs it. A candle burns
in front of the open screen

while the sea churns under the bellies
of fishing boats. I lean across the beds to touch
your arm and your breath quickens.
You startle, towards me, not yet awake—
and full of myself, like the bowl
that harbors its own beginnings, I rumple
your hair—and wait for armistice.

Four

Making Up

Like the apple tree
behind the house
that twists
its withered limbs
out and upward
as if to mime
its lost fruitfulness,
she stands at her sink
to dab on skin cream,
moisten her dry lips
with a pink stick
and tone down the purple
Kool-Aid stripe
a neighbor child has
painted on her
white hair. She squints
into the mirror
with myopic
eyes, then steps
back to let the glaze
of evening sun trans-
late the woman
in the glass
into the girl that
was.

Self-Exam

Out of the tub and Fay inspects
herself: elbow above the left breast,
smooth as an old boulder. Now
the right; her fingers plough west
to east: old ropy flesh but firm enough
for all that. The thumb halts north
of the nipple—what's this?
A fleshy knob? Once more around...
Still there. A niggardly knot, a bulb
buried under the pucker of skin
and no one
    home. She'd thought it
a clean break, leaving him after all those
years—like cruising the fast lane
on the thruway. Gun it, babe, you're on.
Something, of course, could thunder
up behind: a sideswipe by a swaggering
horse van, tractor-trailer flattening
flesh like a stack of cans.
     But maybe
nothing at all—a thousand empty yards
of tar...
    Her mind begs as her fingers
dig.

Breaking the Habit

Here's Ruth in Grand Central Station to meet a lover. The wife is dead and now he is free. He has the ring and Ruth is to wear a white dress—she feels like a rabbit the way the sash bunches out at the back. They met on a blackout ship in a war. You can see how easy it was to make love: the wife back home in the light and Ruth a single girl. In war, he told her, you grab what and when you can—like riding a horse with blinders, reaching for a lodestar. But wars end, and habits outlive the guilts. They met in bars and attic rooms; he talked of a Future. He was *trapped,* he said: *the wife's religion, you see.*

Ruth is early. He is late. And the years she has waited flash past like the crowds in the concourse below, never staying except for a drink, a quick embrace. Like Ruth's kindergarteners hugging goodbye at year's end—then back each fall with new faces. Nothing that stays except confusion (was that Frost?). And there he is! Below. His legs spread wide. The glare from the skylight whitens his balding head, the aquiline nose—she has never seen him from above like this. His mouth opens as he lifts his chin to find her; fingers claw the knot of his skewed tie, red like the shroud of roses he holds in his fleshy hands. Ruth has lived alone since her husband died, no one to ask her *What's for dinner?* tell her to *Wear a white dress* when, God knows, white dresses look ridiculous on a woman of sixty-six. Ruth's color is blue.

Anyway, she was invited for drinks tonight with the woman who moved in next door. Attractive. Single. Her age more or less. Why not? His eyes circle toward her now. He still hasn't seen her. Ruth starts, like a hare caught dozing in sun. Down the steps she races and on to Track 33, squeezes through the car doors—oh the thrill of *a close encounter!* The train hustles out of the station, hurtling Ruth along safe. And out of control.

Seeking Sanctum

Women in the books and magazines
I've been reading lately are all on the look-
out: Ahab's wife on the widow's walk,
scanning the seas for a manic spouse—
himself in search of a mythical whale
while Emma Bovary hunts the male
who would rush her *away* from the waste
of provincial life. Or conflicted
Mary Wollstonecraft in six biographies,
craving romance over self reliance—
at what terrible cost?
     Women for tenure,
a seat in the senate, a night out
to howl on a fence like a feral cat
or watch the psychological film that *he*
can't bear to see. Women, like Woolf,
who lust for a room of their own to write in.
Women wringing their brains
for a lost dream, a windmill of chance—
or like my sister, seeking a like-
minded female.
     Now in my winter walls:
a scrabbling where some hapless
creature is after a bed, a drop of water,
a dry place to give birth. Soon she'll
break through the sheetrock and here we'll be,
eye to I. Do I offer the cat's dish? Clean
flannel sheets, a room with yellow
wallpaper—
     or should I push her out
the door where we'll have to begin all over
again: gnawing and digging, clawing
and scratching, our teeth icicles, rumps bare
to the January squall, our numbed parts knowing
only the panic to crawl somewhere inside.

Passing Place

Five women watch in a bedroom:
one is a midwife, two are neighbors,
a sister. Inside a circle of arms
a mother labors, a husband croons
as he rubs her quavery shoulders.
Candles quicken in a window.
Beyond the light the mother's mother
squats, her hands cramp in her lap.
She pushes as the daughter pushes
but bears no fruit. The daughter
is rich with blood, her flesh,
at the midwife's coaxing, heaves

and splits. A head squeezes through,
the hair, greenish-gold like a raw
peach. A shoulder blossoms, elbows
like bent twigs, the belly, bound
by its lively stem to the matrix, penis,
plump as a worm. Then legs,
centipede-like, but only two—the father
counts the toes. Everyone awed
and smiling, the mother quiet,
father cutting the cord like a boy
unhooking a fish. The child squirms
in his arms; he exults.

The grandmother pictures the day of
her own birthing when she
was the root of life. She pictures her
death. Will five women keep watch?
Will a midwife compass her out through the dark?

Fay Drops In On an Apple Doctor

Fresh cheeked and white-
haired he leans over
her bare breast and they talk
poems. Apparently
he writes a little, a Carlos
Williams. Last week the poem
was about an aunt who
died—it was pancreatic cancer.
He blames the farm she lived on.
He blames the pesticides:
the chlordane, the heptaclor
epoxide. They killed her,
he says, for the money.

Weekends he grows apples,
a dozen organic trees. He gives
the fruit away, he grafts
Granny Smith on to Gingergold,
nine varieties on a single tree:
Gala, Grimes Golden,
Greening, Gravenstein.
The doctor knows alliteration,
he knows about line
breaks—finds one—left
of Fay's nipple. The fingers
pause.

Now they talk endings,
the way a poem comes
like love
to climax, a slow swelling
under the skin, like a worm
burrowing into the core
and the apple
splits.

Mastectomy

Baring the left breast,
all that is precious cast
to the winds the virgins run
the Olympic track. Their toes
squash in and out of the April
ooze, their breath outwhistles
the siren's; the nipples sweat on
the swinging stalks like pink fruits.

Invisible woman, I wait at the side.
Dampness peels away my skin, I
move weightless as fog against
the finish line and beyond
the boundaries of bone.
Defiance wreathes my
wet brow, I lean
into the wind
until I am
wind.

Dancing in the Dark
with a Silver Cane

My brother's cane is a stroke
of lightning spun from a silvery
wrist; the hip he split
falling from a Chinese sky
in a long ago war
he can't stop thinking about
aches on its eddying axis;
he blinds himself to the pain.

The ballroom turns
as he twists, the pale hairs
rise on his glistening skull
as if he's been struck
with his own rod. He croons
along with the band
and his wrecked hip cranks
like a top gone berserk

until the skies are aflame
and he leaps! The chute opens,
sinks through a dusky
hole as the plane careens along
a bloodshot path
and plummets into a house of green tea.

He still hears the dying
as he reels through the ruby dark.

Letting Go

A woman in my high rise apartment
climbed up on the roof to hurl down
a pile of books, dishes, pots,
pillows, hairbrushes, tampons—finally
herself. Before anyone could intervene,
a neighbor said, it flashed past
fourteen windows like trash flung
into a dump, the woman's skull
ground like fishbones into cement.

What she was thinking as she went?
Or was she in some vacuous limbo
like an elevator hurtling downward
from the topmost floor and we hold our
breath till it stops—then stagger
out, dumbfounded, into the lobby.

She never got up, did she, this woman
of thirty-six? She'd had it up *to her eye-
balls* with feckless lovers, she
told the neighbor: landlords,
creditors, foster care supervisors,
kids *like starving cats* fighting over
a stale Sara Lee cupcake. *Get
lost,* the boyfriend snarled
as he slammed the door. And she did.

Sometimes when the sky is iron
from five days of hard rain and some
hate group bans my favorite book,
and no one phones on my birthday—and
somewhere in the world male animals
capture a hundred schoolgirls
and one more woman longing for love

goes down under an avalanche of stone—then

I picture that free-fall from the fourteenth
floor; I draw the drapes, cut
the lights, lapse with a cold whisky-
sour by an open window, and I think,
like that mad lone woman—of letting go.

Remember Pearl Harbor

The collar tightens on my brother's neck as his weak eyes squint to see who's here. He wears the brace, the aide explains, to keep his head from sinking into his lap. His mouth yawns wide as if he sees a ghost—a sound like dry sobs in the throat. The ghost is myself, his younger sister, a school girl while he was flying the Hump, dropping bombs on the enemy.

After the war he came home dashing and jaunty in his flyer's pinks, the leg he'd hurt bailing out of a burning plane only partially healed. Mother and I watched as he shook a pile of stinky socks out of his pack, a snap of himself with a monkey on his shoulder, an arm around a Chinese girl. *You didn't!* Mother cried, and Dan and I laughed. He asked how school was going. *Okay*, I said, my wars too small to relate to a homecoming hero.

For Dan was always the hero: baseball, basketball, theater—drinking in the applause, leaving us sisters in his wake. Years later he danced at my wedding: you'd never know the pain of the hip the way he waved the cane about, a regular Fred Astaire, waltzing with the ladies. We sat up late to hear the war stories, the throb in his voice as he remembered: the camaraderie, the male bonding—as though his wife and children were post-script from a conflict filled with men who danced each day with death. Like the rear gunner of their Bachelor's Quarters B-29, the only one who wouldn't budge when they had to jump. He added something new, I recall: the color of the gunner's eyes as he stared back at Dan through an open bulkhead door. Eyes a flaming pink. At least that's the way Dan saw it. That detail nearly killed me.

His chin rears up like a dog's out of a tight lead; light-blue eyes lock with my earthy brown. His body trembles to push out a word, like the feeble bark of our arthritic collie seeing a cat he knows he can't outrun. *Remember Pearl Harbor* the one-legged man across the room sings, and the aide and I take up the song while Dan's mouth opens and his hands reach for mine.

And I know he is still that cocky young airman inside. He is singing that song in his bones, he is getting ready to stride down the field. To leap up into his plane. *To bang the bejeezus out of the Japs.*

Laundry

Will drops by from his school to say
hello. As though in afterthought, he's
brought his laundry—do I mind?
Too late if I do, but he's my grandson;
made his debut in intensive care—
until he rallied, indigo-eyed and dimpling;

he still has that off-center grin. The canvas
bag arrives on his back like a furled
sail, billows out into fetid hockey socks,
sweaty shirts and boxer shorts
saved up for weeks—I hold my breath
as it all spills out. We chat over tea

and macaroons while the maiden batch
washes; the second as the first
spins dry. I think of my brother, at fourteen,
wheeling across an icy pond—struck
by an errant puck, and Mother trying
to stanch the wound while Dan pleads to *get*

back in the game. So much in play since
then: births, weddings, wars, divorce,
deaths—and all at once, it seems, like laundry
churning in a dryer. I try to seize the day
but before I can get a grip, Will
is layering pants and socks back into the bag.

A hug and he's off to *a masked hop*, he says,
our visit already past tense, like clothing
folded into tidy piles—only a patch of dried
blood on a shirt to tell what happened;
the boys who wore it, sea-changed now
into something clean, sweet—and strange.

This Cold House

The energy man has turned the furnace
off this bleak November day
and wanting to locate leaks in my 1825
farmhouse, the fellow has hooked up
a rig to force air out the door
and let the wind enter the house. Now
the whole outdoors is blowing in,
howling through kitchen and living room,
freezing the study where I sit
with a novel, *Saving the World*.

I'm just trying to save myself—the cost
of fuel has gone through the roof.
A squall might sweep me out
of my chair and into the cracks
the man insists are everywhere: attic
and basement, under the sink and stove,
behind the silverware drawer where mice
squeeze in. It might be an exorcism.
I'm vacuuming out a houseful
of ghosts: an errant lover, a vengeful
ex-spouse. I throw on shawls, a couple
of cats—furs my forebears wore
in their drafty caves. I'm hunkering back

into niche and quoin, into earthy tunnels
the storm can't reach. I'm feeding on
fat to keep the blood moving through all
the rooms of this old house: I'm
a snow goose fleeing toward summer's heat,
a curled-up fetus, snug in the womb.
Safe from a world gone haywire.

Two-Way Glass

If I had my easel I would sketch
four women at lunch in a mountain
farmhouse where the knives
click on the chipped plates
and talk flutters in and out on forks:
a friend's new grandchild,
myself content after a time of grieving.
My daughter nesting again
the way time overlaps like quilts
tossed on a pumpkin pine bed.
Outside, a feeder swings
from a golden oak and just after
the carrot-raisin salad a lady

cardinal jabs at the windowpane
with her bold red beak; black eyes
fix the eight inside as if
this is a two-way glass: a woman
out in the cold fall afternoon
and staring in at those four old
birds at lunch: all of them
laughing at the greedy rebel looking
to trade her sunflower seeds
for cool lemon pound cake.

Reprieve

Birds bob at the feeder like swimmers
treading water, filling their bellies
before the storm. Thirty inches or more,
we're told, schools about to close
and shoppers scrambling for food, candles—
and time. Time coming to a stop.
                              And all
the things I've neglected to do in my long-
short life welling up in my head:
pilot a plane, learn Chinese, Arabic,
chess, anthropology, a doctorate
in Gaelic. Peace Corps in Ghana. Or
simply meditate—*om-mm-mmm*
for hours, on end.
                      It starts at twilight:
whispering snow, white-washing
the windows, rushing past
like the last sixty years, sweeping the heart
with wind, with night-long sheets
and shrouds of snow.
                      I breathe in
my childhood, awe of the night; my hair
goes dark again, skin like polished ice
on a sheltered pond. *Let me go on
sleeping, Mom.*
                      Dawn brings sky-
lit towers of white. Nothing to splinter
the silence, only steeps of white.
White quiet as drifting clouds,
white turreted castles, white walls thawing
in sun.
                      While inside on the breakfast table
a birthday card. My sister's gift
of a silver watch—already ticking.

Five

Acts of Balance

The only position I could ever do
correctly in yoga class was the *corpse.*
I would close my eyes, collapse
on the floor and the teacher
wouldn't have to shove an elbow, knee,
or ankle into a place it couldn't –

or wouldn't go until one day she said
to stand on one leg and I was about
to fall when someone to my left touched
my shoulder with a finger; a woman
to my right did the same, the barest touch,
and I touched them, and eight women

on eight feet stood in a circle and not one
of us fell. I recall, too, getting up in the cold
dark for the sunrise at Bryce Canyon,
standing beside a gawky man in glasses.
A dozen strangers, we slowly massed
together, arms linked, until we were one

amorphous whole. The sun rose, like a minister
blessing her flock and I was warm,
like this cool March day on Champlain Bridge
when the smallest puff of wind might send me off-
balance and spinning into a void…
and *he,* with a single word, holds me up.

Ruth in my Kitchen Snapping Beans

Ruth sits in my kitchen snapping
beans. It's all she can do now.
She can't stuff a turkey—
you need balance to do that:
it's like shoving your body
through a tunnel in wet sand,
you're headed for Greece.
Ruth can't set the table—who can

juggle ten plates with a cane?
I think of an egret
shuffling about while feeding
like it's had one too many.
So Ruth sits and snaps beans.
They shoot off like drunks

banging a target, one bean bops
the cat on its pink nose,
one lands on a faded snap-
shot of two young girls at camp:
there's Ruth in her red suit
in that cold Vermont lake—

God it was cold! Me hugging
my chest and Ruth in there
splashing away, her arms
and legs so crazy in the freezing
water you think she'll lift

right out, her stick legs
trailing like kite strings, her
feathers wild-spread in the wind.

Couplings

Barefoot on the cut grass the engineer
lays track. He clamps together the rails
until the circle completes: an oblong
sphere of brass like a mini hi-way splitting
a vale where my grand-nephew and I
hang out to watch. Careful as a midwife
holding a newborn, he sets the steam
locomotive on the rails, hooks up
the red freight car and sends them
on their way.
        We listen to the whistle,
the clackety wheels as they
racket along the curve—
as the wheels encounter a root
then leap the track—
        Hey! Robbie shouts.
The engineer drops to his knees to shore up
the earth, cradle the cars and set them on course
the way his fingers ease my fears for the May-
December bond that has lately been
my world.
        The train coasts the rails
until it is almost out of sight—and
back it reels, careening
round the curve as smooth and sweet
as a couple racing the sun
with clasped hands, eyes on a filmy sky
as though he and she are everything
and all these flaws, knots and roots
straws in a wash.

Late Shift at Green Pastures

Ruth is in love. She can only whisper
the news but the room quickens
as if struck by lightning; her neck flushes
pink, saliva drips from the split
crease of her lip. I wipe her damp chin,
I stoop to the wary ear: I say
Who's the lucky guy, Ruth? But she
holds a shaky finger to her nose
like a pendulum nodding in an antique clock;
her eyes wax black: she's a sealed
pitcher with a broken lip. She's the girl
with a crush on the teacher who speaks her
name, the rose with the sucking bee,
the bittersweet hugging the butterfly bush.
Pee spreads thick and warm in the sheets.
I think, Ruth is in love—and I am, too.
Her lady friend comes to stroke her hair
while Ruth gazes deep into her face
and her eyes roll in like a foggy
morning after a night of teeming rain.

Fay Looks Back on the Ambivalence of Sisters

There is something about sisters that tugs at the gut—whether blood kin or a cluster of women sharing a pallet, a passion—a part of one another. Like the three mythical Graeae siblings who shared a single tooth, a single eye. And when the Greek warrior Perseus stole that eye, they were forced to aid in the beheading of their sister Medusa.

Consider Elizabeth, who at age twenty in 1553, wrote to her Catholic sister Mary: "It seems I now am, without cause, to go unto the Tower." Her diamond scratched its protest into a window glass: *"nothing proved can be."* Still, she was borne across the prison moat in a night dress. In the end though, Queen Mary couldn't bring herself to take a sister's head. On Mary's death, Elizabeth mourned: "The laws of nature moveth me to sorrow for my sister."

There was scant sorrow on Elizabeth's part for her "sister-cousin," Mary Queen of Scots, rival to the throne. Crucifix in hand, Mary "laid herself upon the block" and the sword whistled down (twice) to split her neck. The queen's lips "stirred up and down," a witness said, "almost a quarter of an hour after her death." A protest from the soul?

My sister Ruth, who once argued as a young woman that she had "no voice, no listeners," went more obligingly to her death: "sans teeth...sans taste, sans everything," as Shakespeare wrote. For me it was a frenetic day of holiday cooking, cleaning—a panic of company—when a nurse phoned from Green Pastures to say my sister was feeling anxious. Her woman friend away. Ruth "asking for me—could I come?"

"Yes," but I postponed my visit to the following day when nephews would arrive and bring her to us. How could I manage any sooner?

Too late.

The night after the memorial service I relived my sister's last visit: the wheelchair in my nephews' hands lunging over the doormat, Ruth hoisted across their locked arms like a frozen sheet. The boys wrestling the mute weight until the woodstove thawed it.

"*It*," I whispered, horrified, as though I'd turned her into some kind of triadic, archaic Graeae sister.

And through the Parkinson mask came the murmur: "Sorry. Damn. But wha' can I do t' *help*?"

Oh, Ruth.

Changing Direction

This morning the sun
tints Camel's Hump
salmon-pink, a new day

defrosting the world.
Under the shelf
of Adirondacks

the lake lies gray
and frozen, its
passage north inter-

rupted by ice.
Once it belonged
to the sea:

Abenakis tell
of drowned bodies
preserved in the salty

hollows of whale
bellies—long ago
Jonahs on moonless

journeys to the East.
Ruth has gone West.
She lies perfectly

still in the white bed,
her knees angled
sharp as the ribs

of winter mountains.
Under the drawn sheet
her mute hands appear

to hold something
the way my man's
fingers tighten

on his iphone when he
falls asleep; he'll hang on
as if it warns of some

new ice age and he has
to know how to escape,
if he has any choice.

The dead have no such
fears. If the floor
of the Champlain Valley

continues to rise,
geologists say,
a thousand centuries

will see the lake
reverse its flow to south.
It won't be long, Ruth:

the years will pass
like the swift
descent of the gray sperm

whale into the breath-
less sea. I'll listen
for your voice.

Fay Frees Three Pounds of Heroine

Wildfire pinks, columbine, and yellow stargrass
on the back seat, Ruth on the floor next
to the gear shift and Fay careens into the meetinghouse
graveyard—a cop car closing in on her tailgate
with a siren shriek that would freeze old Ulysses
to his mast. He slips her a ticket. Not a speck
of empathy in the sun-glazed eyes. *So what's the hurry?*
Folks here can wait, huh? Hands like slabs
of white fish slap the rim of the Volvo window.
Squinting eyes discover the purple urn.

Three pounds of heroine here, sir. (Ruth always
loved a little double entendre.) Fay holds
the urn to her chest as the cop leans in close
and sniffs. Mistress of permutation, Ruth used to trans-
form her kindergarten pupils into gold and purple
butterflies—even the fat ones could fly. A girl who
walked the balance beam on fingertips,
Ruth hadn't a tibia left in the end supple enough
to bend, the Parkinson's muscles too rigid
for a ramble in the woods, her tongue a dried apricot.

The dead don't pay, Fay says as she rips
up the ticket, tips the urn, and grainy bits of ash
whip off among the monuments of time
like an old heart riding the wind, riding the yellow
stargrass, the wild fire pinks. Riding
lickety-split over the power line.

Fay Enters Armageddon

She sweeps across the lawn
to meet him, one-breasted woman
of seventy-two, broad brimmed
hat riding low over an auburn wig,
Queen Anne's lace in her sinewy arms
and pink and white snapdragons.
He waits by a peony bush, gold rings
in his sweaty palm, white duck
legs that won the '82 Croquet Marathon
rooted in the grass like a wicket;
his glasses flash in the sun.
                              On she goes,
Vermont Venus in size eleven
sandals: toes dazzle pink, the sun
dimples her elbows, eyes glint green
in the damp pouches of skin. She's
had it all: family (or lack of), verses
in the lit mags, thirty acres
of farmland ripe as old pond water,
her own way in a house
without husband; if the cat howled
at two in the morning, it was Fay who
forgot to put it out.
                        The fiddle
drives her forward, she's almost
there: the sun irons him into a silhouette;
her mind is a-blaze like his spectacled
eyes. She ploughs into his presence (a-
mazing Fay); she's taller than he
by a thumb; the wind drums in her ears,
a calf bellows in the pen. The dobbin
canters along the fence—she'll catch him as he comes.

Riding the Staten Island Ferry in a Thunderstorm

We're only on it for the excitement, we
elders: the thrill of riding the East
River like a bucking horse in driving
rain, lightning flash—and maybe
a hurricane. A woman wants to *turn back.*
Swim, then, her man says. Dime-sized
hail dices the waves, but we've come a day-
long trek on Amtrak to see Ms. Liberty
and there she is! to starboard,
arm thrust high as if ready to shake a fist
at anyone who'd knock her off base.
Beyond her crown, the sun is a red hot coal.
A fireboat, just off-island, spews out
ropes of water as if in salute.   We dock and
the crowd shoves off. But there's little
to see now on Staten Island and so
we veer about, like riding *back and forth all night*
on the ferry. The poet's boat, she wrote,
smelled like a stable, horses below—but I smell
only an onion sandwich, ketchup and pickles.
The wind comes cold and thunder
grumbles over in Queens; lightning forks
the roofs. Milady lights her torch
as we pass. Night falls on the water. High rise
windows wink, a half moon squints
through a veil of fog. *We were very merry,* yes,
but Millay's sun was young, and ours
is beginning to set. It's time now to disembark:
Get your coat. Got your subway pass?

*★Italicized lines from Edna St Vincent Millay's Recuerdo: Last line a riff on a line
by Ruth Stone*

CPSIA information can be obtained at www.ICGtesting.com
Printed in the USA
BVOW08s1846150516

448152BV00003BA/179/P